D1048543

Simple Science Sermons
For Big And Little Kids

Guy Stewart

CSS Publishing Company, Inc., Lima, Ohio

SIMPLE SCIENCE SERMONS FOR BIG AND LITTLE KIDS

Copyright © 1998 by
CSS Publishing Company, Inc.
Lima, Ohio

All rights reserved. No part of this publication may be reproduced in any manner whatso-
ever without the prior permission of the publisher, except in the case of brief quotations
embodied in critical articles and reviews. Inquiries should be addressed to: Permissions,
CSS Publishing Company, Inc., P.O. Box 4503, Lima, Ohio 45802-4503.

Scripture quotations are from the *New Revised Standard Version of the Bible*, copyright
1989 by the Division of Christian Education of the National Council of the Churches of
Christ in the USA. Used by permission.

ISBN 0-7880-1294-0   PRINTED IN U.S.A.

To Liz, my love and strength;
To Josh and Mary, my joy;
To Richard and Ruth, I wish they could have seen this;
To Chuck and Pat, the first to believe in me.

Table Of Contents

Introduction

I've been a science teacher for fifteen years. I love science. I also love the Lord. Combining two very different — and sometimes antagonistic — endeavors gave me a chance to make a bridge between the two. Children love science — the popularity of shows like *Newton's Apple*, *Beakman's World*, and *Bill Nye, The Science Guy* is evidence of that.

The tone of these "sermons" is light, bantering, and informational. I use the experiment — or more properly, the demonstration — the way an illusionist or "magician" uses her tricks. As I talk about serious things, like salvation or walking with Jesus, I'm doing something with my hands. The aim of the demonstration is to illustrate more clearly a principle of Scripture.

I hope that with this book you can do the same. These twenty demonstrations are only a beginning. Any science trick or experiment can be linked to God's Word. God is the Author of both. At the end of the book you'll find a short resource list. Search these books and search the Scripture. Then put them together and create your own Science Sermons!

Some things you might want to have on hand:

A) White lab coat

B) Safety goggles (Get both the dumbest-looking pair and a pair of the "sunglasses" type.)

C) A low table (about 18 inches) (I sit on the floor when I do my demonstrations. The short table allows me to have working space and to keep things out of the reach of toddlers.)

D) If you have access to "laboratory equipment," use it. A beaker, an Erlenmeyer flask, and a 100-milliliter graduated cylinder aren't essential, but they DO make measuring easier and they add to your "scientific atmosphere."

E) Lots of towels! Some of these demonstrations can get messy.

F) A bag to carry everything in up to your demonstration spot. It helps to increase the suspense and lets you chat longer as you "unload" your equipment.

G) An electric hot plate

H) PRACTICE! Don't expect things to go well if you don't try the demonstration at least once! With science, as with everything, Murphy's Law prevails: "Anything that CAN go wrong, WILL go wrong," especially when you're doing the demonstration for children.

1

Oobleck And Temptation

The Verse
Hebrews 4:15: "For we do not have a high priest who is unable to sympathize with our weaknesses, but we have one who in every respect has been tempted as we are — yet without sin."

What You Need
1 box of cornstarch
1 pie tin
water
towels

Some Ideas Of What To Say
(Begin by unloading bag.) "Can anyone here tell me what the word 'temptation' means? *(Most won't know, but probe for a few answers.)* It's a good thing you don't know! If you already knew, I'd have to pack up and leave. I'm here to show you something that will help you understand what temptation is.

"I've got some stuff here — anyone know what cornstarch is? *(Pour about one third of the contents of a full box into the pie tin. By now, you have their full attention.)* Cornstarch comes from corn plants. People usually use it to cook with. But I'm going to show you something else you can do with it. *(Add about a half cup [100 milliliters] of water to the cornstarch. PRACTICE ahead of time so you have some idea how much water to add. You need to reach a stage where there's no 'free' water floating on top of the oobleck.)* What I've just made here is called oobleck. I think it's called oobleck because the first people that saw it and touched it said, 'Oooo! Bleck!' *(Play with it. Allow it to drop through your fingers. Allow everyone to say 'ick.')* Pretty nasty stuff, eh? This is such nasty

9

stuff that — well, I can think of a few nasty things I could do with it. Like, put it in my sister's hair. *(Fake this with one of the children — but be careful!)* Another neat thing about oobleck is that it is a plastic — not the plastic that they make toys out of. It's a substance that isn't a solid OR a liquid, but both. So I could break out a piece *(break a piece out of the mess)*, and roll it into a ball *(do it)*. And if I dropped it on the table, it would bounce, then ooze. I could throw it, bonk someone in the head, and slime them all at the same time! *(Do this to the table a couple of times.)* In fact, oobleck is such nasty stuff that it seems to be CALLING me to do nasty things with it. *(Do a 'far off call' here, illustrating the 'call' oobleck has on you. My oobleck called me to grab my pastor by the lapels of his dark suit — and leave behind nice white marks!)* Now here's the tough question: If this nasty stuff was around in Jesus' time, would he have thrown it in his sister's hair? *(Pause)* Would he have slimed the rabbi's coat? *(Pause)* NO! Jesus wouldn't have. He would have kept away from doing something nasty. He would have resisted temptation. Temptation is something that seems to call to you. You know it's wrong, but for most of us we do it anyway. The Bible says that Jesus was tempted, but he didn't sin. Oobleck would be calling him just like it called to me. But instead of doing something nasty, Jesus DIDN'T do it. Because Jesus knows all about temptation, he gives us the strength to resist it."

The Science Behind The Sermon

The cornstarch and water make a strange fluid — called a plastic or a non-Newtonian fluid. It behaves the opposite of water: when you put pressure on it, it becomes THICKER rather than getting out of the way. As soon as the pressure's off, it thins out again. Long molecules of starch tighten and hold their shape under pressure. They loosen up and flow when the pressure is released.

2

Phenolphthalein And Forgiveness

The Verse
Isaiah 1:18: " 'Come now, let us argue it out,' says the Lord. 'Though your sins are like scarlet, they shall be like snow; though they are red like crimson, they shall become like wool.' "

What You Need
1 mayonnaise-sized jar with lid
bottle of ammonia (non-sudsing)
bottle of CLEAR vinegar
measuring cup
measuring spoons
phenolphthalein (This is a clear liquid known as an "acid/base indicator." The only way to get it is to find someone you know who teaches high school/junior high/middle school chemistry. Ask to borrow the bottle. If you can't get the whole bottle, ask to borrow about 100 milliliters. It is considered a poison, so be careful.)

(NOTE: The difficulty of getting hold of phenolphthalein is far outweighed by the dramatic effect this demonstration has. If you can get it, do!)

Some Ideas Of What To Say
(Begin by unloading bag.) "What is sin? *(Entertain any reasonable answers.)* The Greek word for sin means 'missing the mark.' Kind of like, when you shoot an arrow at a target and miss the whole thing. Or if you throw a basketball and miss the basket. The Bible says in Romans that everybody sins. That means that everybody misses the mark.

11

"What mark do you think they're talking about? *(Pour a cup of vinegar into the jar. Also entertain any reasonable answers to your question.)* The mark — the center of the target or the basketball hoop — was set up by God. We were supposed to be perfect. How many of you here are perfect? *(You hope no one will raise his hand! Add about three tablespoons of phenolphthalein.)* Good, I'm glad to see I'm not the only sinner here. But you know, even though we are sinners, God can take away our sins. How can he do that? *(Jesus' sacrifice on the cross and resurrection.)*

"Jesus took away our sins by dying on the cross and rising again from the dead. Because of Jesus, we are perfect in God's eyes. In Isaiah it says, 'Though your sins are like scarlet, they shall be like snow; though they are red like crimson, they shall become like wool.' That means that our sins were so bad that they made us look bright red in God's eyes. *(Add one cup plus one teaspoon of ammonia to the jar. The solution will turn bright pink.)* Our sins look like this to God. But because of Jesus, our sins are forgiven. *(Add two teaspoons of vinegar and the liquid will turn white or clear again!)* Does that mean we can go ahead and do whatever we want? *(Add just over two teaspoons of ammonia. The solution should turn pink again. You can go back and forth as many times as you like.)* Jesus has forgiven our sins and taken them away! Hallelujah! The Bible says, 'Come now, let us argue it out, says the Lord. Though your sins are like scarlet, they shall be like snow; though they are red like crimson, they shall become like wool.'"

The Science Behind The Sermon
An acid/base indicator like phenolphthalein changes color from clear to pink over a very narrow range of acidity or "acidness." Vinegar is an acid. Ammonia is a base. When there is more ammonia (or base), phenolphthalein is clear. When there is more acid, it turns pink.

3

An Electric Pickle And The Holy Spirit

The Verse
Acts 2:1-3, 38-39: "When the day of Pentecost had come, they were all together in one place. And suddenly from heaven there came a sound like the rush of a violent wind, and it filled the entire house where they were sitting. Divided tongues, as of fire, appeared among them, and a tongue rested on each of them ... Peter said to them, 'Repent, and be baptized every one of you in the name of Jesus Christ so that your sins may be forgiven; and you will receive the Gift of the Holy Spirit.' "

What You Need
an old lamp cord, cut off from the lamp (Split the end so you have about a foot's worth of two wires. Strip three inches of plastic from the ends.)
2 nails (flat heads, about four inches long)
large pickle
an outlet near your place of demonstration
(This is best done in a darkened room.)

Some Ideas Of What To Say
(Begin by unloading bag.) "What's Pentecost? *(Entertain reasonable answers.)* Pentecost was the day that the Holy Spirit descended from God and touched the disciples. It was a very surprising day for them. I'm pretty sure some of them were scared. I guess I'd have been scared if I was standing around and suddenly a tongue of fire appeared on my head. *(Put pickle in the middle of the table.)* I'm going to try to give you an idea today of how startling those tongues of fire must have been to the disciples. Remember, it was something that had never happened before. They should have been

13

expecting it because Jesus told them he'd be sending the Comforter (John 14:26). But that wasn't what they were thinking about. *(Take out cord, wrap the nails.)* They were thinking about their heads, which appeared to be on fire. I think I can give you an idea of HOW surprised they were by doing this little demonstration. *(This can be dangerous. KEEP OUT OF REACH OF CHILDREN. Stand back yourself. Insert nails into pickle.)* How many of you have seen an electric pickle? *(If anyone has, ask him to keep a secret as to what's about to happen.)* What do you think will happen when I plug my pickle in? *(Any reasonable answer. Ask an assistant to dim the lights. Plug in the pickle. Keep your hand on the plug. The pickle will do nothing at first. Then you'll hear a sizzle. Then the INSIDE of the pickle will light up. Unplug it. You'll notice an interesting smell. So will everyone else!)* How many of you were surprised that the pickle lit up? How surprised do you think the disciples were when their heads lit up? Our God is a god of surprises. He'll never let us down because he's given us the Holy Spirit — maybe not as dramatically as he gave it to the first disciples at Pentecost, but he HAS promised us the Holy Spirit. God always keeps his promises! Amen? Amen!"

The Science Behind The Sermon

Electricity is conducted or passed through water very easily. Salt water conducts electricity better than fresh water. Because pickles are made with salt water, the electric current passes fairly easily through the pickle. The current "burns" the carbohydrates in the pickle, and that's what produces the light inside the pickle — and the smell.

4

White Powder, Suffering, And Surprise

The Verse
1 Peter 4:12-13: "Beloved, do not be surprised at the fiery ordeal that is taking place among you to test you, as though something strange were happening to you. But rejoice insofar as you are sharing Christ's sufferings, so that you may also be glad and shout for joy when his glory is revealed."

What You Need
vinegar (cover the label with a large sign label that says "ACID")
4 jars (filled ahead of time with one-third cup each of the following:
    BLEACHED flour
    baking soda
    sugar
    salt
food coloring

Some Ideas Of What To Say
    (Unload your bag and read the verse.) "Can anyone tell me what that verse means? *(It is doubtful that anyone can. Then ask the congregation, followed by the pastor or some other knowledgeable individual. Arrange beforehand for them to play 'dumb.')* That's a hard verse to understand, but I think this little, possibly DANGEROUS, demonstration will help today. *(Emphasize DANGEROUS. This demonstration is EMPHATICALLY NOT dangerous. For the purpose of the illustration, however, you want the kids to THINK so. Set out the four jars.)* I've got four powders here. They look pretty much the same. *(Take out vinegar.)* But only one of these powders will react with this acid. In fact, the one powder that will react with it will ... Well, I'm not going to say. I'm going to need four very brave volunteers to help me with this today.

(Choose them. Give each one a jar. Have them stand, facing the congregation. Make sure the baking soda jar is the LAST jar you add vinegar to. Add a couple of drops of red food coloring to each. Use one of your science props like the beaker, Erlenmeyer flask, or graduated cylinder to painstakingly measure out about 50 milliliters [one-third cup] of vinegar. As you prepare to pour the vinegar, make sure you ask several times if the child is ready. Build this up. As each child's reaction is a dud, the tension will build to the last one ...) So, it looks like you might be the one. *(Start to pour, then stop. Offer the child your safety goggles. Insist that she take them.)* You're sure you're ready? *(Finally pour it. You'll get a fizzing reaction. Not terribly exciting, but not too bad, either.)* So, how does it feel to be a scientist? *(Take whatever reaction you get; try and keep this light.)* Now, can you tell me what this demonstration has to do with the Bible verse? *(They probably can't. Ask others.)* Remember the verse said that you shouldn't be surprised at the problems you'll have. Jesus suffered, and so will you. I warned everyone to expect something. Over and over I warned people, so that when the baking soda and vinegar fizzed up, no one was really surprised. Well, Jesus told us many times that we would have trouble, because we don't really belong in this world. We belong in heaven. So when we DO have trouble, we need to rejoice. Rejoice doesn't mean we have to be happy — rejoicing is knowing that God is sending us somewhere new and exciting. He's already suffered. We will, too. But he always loves us and he's got PLANS for us. Good plans!"

The Science Behind The Sermon

Baking soda and vinegar react because one is a base and the other is an acid. They violently exchange parts, releasing carbon dioxide gas (that stuff that makes soda fizz) until all that's left is a salt.

5

A Balloon, A Book, Pressure, And Satan

The Verse
James 4:7-8a: "Submit yourselves therefore to God. Resist the devil, and he will flee from you. Draw near to God, and He will draw near to you...."

What You Need
balloons
a few large, thin, wide books (large format children's books like the *Where's Waldo* books work well) wrapped in a paper that says "The Bible"
black permanent marker

Some Ideas Of What To Say
(Begin by unloading bag.) "What does it mean to 'submit'? *(Accept any reasonable answers.)* Submit means to turn control over to someone or something. For example, the book of James in the Bible tells us we're supposed to submit to God. So that would mean that we're supposed to turn over control of our lives to God. Right after those words, James tells us to 'resist the Devil.' What does 'resist' mean? *(Same ...)* When you resist something, you stand against it. When your mother says, 'It's time to go to bed,' what do you do? *(Expect most of them to say 'go to bed.' Some of the older ones will catch on though.)* This demonstration will show you what happens when we resist the Devil — with Jesus' help. *(Blow up several balloons. Ask the children to hold on to them. Hold up the books with the Bible covers.)* The Bible is God's word to us. When the Devil tries to tempt us, we can use God's word to resist that temptation. How can we do that? *(By memorizing Scripture.)* So when the Devil tries to tempt us, we can say Bible verses and then tell him to go away. Good. Now I'm going to show you how science

17

proves that God's word will help us to resist the Devil. *(Hand a balloon and a book to one of the children.)* This balloon is going to be you. *(Draw a face on the balloon, preferably a silly face.)* Take the book, put it on the balloon, sit on it, and try to pop the balloon. *(Clear an area for the child to do this. It will be extremely difficult to break the balloon. In my experience, if nothing sharp pierces the balloon, it WON'T pop. I've done this myself, and with high quality balloons; even an adult has difficulty breaking the balloon — if at all. PRACTICE THIS ONE!!!)* You can think of the balloon as YOU. Think of your backside as the pressure Satan puts on you. Satan tries to get us to sin. He tries to make us do bad things. How can we ever keep from doing wrong? We can 'resist temptation.' When God's word is living in our hearts, we can resist temptation and the Devil will run away from us very fast."

The Science Behind The Sermon

The large book distributes the weight of the person over a larger area of the balloon than usual. A balloon that isn't completely inflated has a lot of "give" in it. When the pressure of the person sitting on the book and balloon is spread over such a large area, the balloon has enough elasticity to stretch without popping.

6

Oil And Water And Baby Moses

The Verse
Exodus 2:3: "When she could hide him no longer she got a papyrus basket for him, and plastered it with bitumen and pitch...."

What You Need
vegetable oil
water
blue food color
2 liter soda bottle
funnel (optional)
small basket of woven reeds

Some Ideas Of What To Say
  (Begin by unloading bag.) "How many of you have seen a baby? How many of you have HELD a baby? How many of you have seen a baby floating in a basket in a river? Back in the very, very olden days, when the Egyptians were building their pyramids, a princess found a baby floating in the weeds of a river. *(Set up the bottle with the funnel.)* Does anyone know who I'm talking about? *(Most kids will know by now.)* So my question is this: *(Hold up basket.)* How did the baby manage to float down a river in something like this without sinking? *(Acknowledge anyone who says that Moses' basket was bigger.)* That's only part of the answer. In fact, there was some pretty complicated science going on in the basket that floated baby Moses into Egyptian history. What was something else? *('Reeds float.')* That's another part of the answer. But what about what Moses' mom did to the basket? Before she even put Moses in the basket, what did she do? The Bible says she covered the basket over with tar and pitch. She did that for two reasons. *(Pour the colored water into the bottle and let it settle.)*

19

The main reason was to plug up all the holes in the basket. (Peek through a hole in your basket.) But it also helped that oil, tar, pitch, and other things like that are LIGHTER than water and are WATERPROOF — which means water can't soak through them. And they float. *(Add the oil slowly to the water mixture and cap the bottle tightly.)* The combination of floating reeds, the tar and pitch plugging the holes in the basket, the size of the basket, and the floatability of reeds and oil kept the baby Moses on top of the water until the Pharaoh's daughter pulled him out of the water. *(Play with the oil/water by gently tilting it from side to side.)* It was no accident that oil floats on water. When God made the universe, he planned all sorts of things to happen. The fact that oil floats on water is just one of the many ways God has taken care of us and our world."

The Science Behind The Sermon

The density (how closely together molecules are packed in a substance) of vegetable oil is somewhat less than that of water, so the oil floats.

7

Tornado Tubes And Job

The Verse
Job 1:18-19; 42:10-12: "While he was still speaking, another came and said, 'Your sons and your daughters were eating and drinking wine in their eldest brother's house, and suddenly a great wind came across the desert, struck the four corners of the house, and it fell on the young people, and they are dead; I alone have escaped to tell you.' " * "And the Lord restored the fortunes of Job when he had prayed for his friends; and the Lord gave Job twice as much as he had before ... And the Lord blessed the latter days of Job more than his beginning...."

What You Need
a "tornado tube" (usually available at a science museum, large school supply store, or by ordering from a scientific supply catalogue)
2 empty, CLEAR two-liter soda bottles
about 1 liter of water (a little over a quart, or half a pitcher)
food coloring
funnel

(NOTE: Most children will have seen a tornado tube. The point of this sermon is to give them some new thoughts on it.)

Some Ideas Of What To Say
    (Begin by unloading bag.) "Most of you have seen one of these. But some of you may not have watched someone put it together or heard an explanation of what happens. *(Read the first part of the passage through the *.)* Can anyone tell me what that 'great wind' might have been? *(Most will say 'tornado,' though some may add 'hurricane' or 'straight line winds' if they've had experience with*

21

them.) It was very likely a tornado. *(Pour water into one of the bottles. Add a few drops of food coloring.)* Job was a man who made God very happy. He did everything he was supposed to do. He was a good man. So Satan went to God and told him that if God would take away Job's things, Job would hate God. God said, 'Go ahead. Job will love me.' Job ended up losing all the things he had. When Job still loved God, Satan said that if Job got sick, he would hate God. Satan made Job very sick. Finally, Job's friends told him he must have done something terrible — because they thought God was punishing Job! Finally, God talked to Job *(Screw on second bottle.)* Most of you have seen a tornado tube. Once I turn it upside down and give a swirl, *(do it)* I get a tornado in a bottle. The water is going around so fast that it makes a tiny air tube in the very middle of the tornado. As the water goes into the bottom bottle, it pushes the air out and up to the top bottle. If that didn't happen, the tornado tube wouldn't work. The water and the air have to trade places to make it work. *(Watch until it runs through once.)* Back to the story: Job stays close to God and, in the end, God gives everything back to him. He has a new family and gets even more of his fortune back. *(Flip bottle and swirl again.)* I use the tornado tube to remind me of what happened to Job — and to remind me of how much God loves us. Whenever you look at a tornado tube, remember how much God loved Job and how much God loves you."

The Science Behind The Sermon

The tornado tube is a simple device that produces a dramatic effect. The explanation is given above as well as on the tornado tube's package.

8

Flowers And Fear

The Verse
Matthew 6:27-30: " 'And can any of you by worrying add a single hour to your span of life? And why do you worry about clothing? Consider the lilies of the field, how they grow; they neither toil nor spin, yet I tell you, even Solomon in all his glory was not clothed like one of these. But if God so clothes the grass of the field, which is alive today and tomorrow is thrown into the oven, will he not much more clothe you — you of little faith?' "

What You Need
scissors
black construction paper
a house plant
tape
one week prep time

Prep Time (One Week Before Using Sermon)
For this one, you'll need one week of prep time. Take a large house plant (like a geranium) and, using the black construction paper and tape, cover one of the leaves completely. Leave the plant alone for a week. Do NOT open it. The chlorophyll that makes leaves green will break down in the colored leaf and will make the leaf look pale.

Some Ideas Of What To Say
(Begin by unloading your bag.) "How many of you have been worried? What makes you worry? Have any of you ever been lost? Being lost makes me worry. *(Relate an incident where you were worried. DO NOT bring it to a conclusion! Leave it hanging for the time being. Point to plant.)* I brought this plant with me to show

you something God has taught me. What do you suppose I have hidden under this paper? *(Accept any reasonable answers. Cut the paper away.)* This leaf has been covered for about a week. What happened to it? *(Accept any reasonable answers.)* Why aren't the other leaves like this? What could this leaf have been missing? *(Sunlight.)* Because it wasn't in the sun, the green stuff in the leaf — it's called chlorophyll — disappeared. How do you suppose the chlorophyll got there? *(Steer the conversation toward God inventing the chlorophyll and putting it in the plants.)* Does the plant have to do anything to make or keep its chlorophyll? No. It just sits in the sun. It doesn't do anything. God has taken care of everything for the plant. The plant only has problems when it gets blocked from the sun. *(Lean forward confidentially.)* Does this plant ever worry? No. Jesus, who is the Son of God, takes care of it. This flower never worries and it stays in the sun. And the Bible says, 'Consider the lilies of the field, how they grow; they neither toil nor spin, yet I tell you, even Solomon in all his glory was not clothed like one of these.' God takes care of the plants. But without the sun, the plant doesn't do very well. You and I are like the plant. Jesus is like the sun in the sky. He's the Son of God. When we get out of his light — or don't read the Bible and pray — we start to look like this sick leaf. But when we read the Bible and pray, God hears us and we get closer to him. *(Finish your worry story.)* Jesus will take care of us! Praise God!"

The Science Behind The Sermon

A chemical called chlorophyll gives plants their green color. It is the chlorophyll that changes sunlight into food that the plant needs. Cutting the leaf off from the sunlight made the leaf stop producing chlorophyll. Eventually the leaf would die and fall off. However, exposing the leaf to the sun again will bring it back to life.

9

Soft Eggshells And Soft Hearts

The Verse
Ezekiel 11:19-20: "I will give them one heart, and put a new spirit within them; I will remove the heart of stone from their flesh and give them a heart of flesh, so that they may follow my statutes and keep my ordinances and obey them. Then they shall be my people, and I will be their God."

What You Need
2 raw eggs, in shell
2 jars with lids (egg needs to fit in each one!)
clear vinegar
(Three days ahead of time, place one egg in a jar and completely cover it with vinegar. Leave it alone. At the end of three days, the shell will be gone and only the soft, tough membrane underneath it will remain.)

Some Ideas Of What To Say
(Begin by unloading bag. Keep the finished product hidden by covering it with a towel.) "Is anyone here stubborn? *(Feign surprise.)* It's a good thing I'M not stubborn. In fact, I'm probably the best person around this church! I'm probably so good that I don't need anybody. I don't even need God! *(Play this for all the comic relief it's worth.)* Is there anyone that would disagree that I'm the best person in this church? *(Again feign surprise.)* Do you suppose God would disagree? God's people, the Israelites, had the same problem I was just having. They thought they were just fine without God. God saw that they were like this and he said that they had 'hard hearts.' *(Pick up egg.)* Can I have one or two of you touch this? Is it hard? *(It will be. Gently place it in the jar.)* But God is a God of great miracles. He told the Israelites that he could take their

hard hearts — their hearts of stone — and turn them soft, make them into hearts of muscle again. *(Pour in vinegar and tightly seal jar.)* That certainly seems impossible, doesn't it? But I can show you a real-life example of how you can change something that is very hard, like this eggshell, into something soft. *(Swirl vinegar and study the jar.)* This particular experiment takes three days to do, so I did it ahead of time. *(Uncover the other jar with the finished experiment in it.)* The vinegar in this jar ate up all the calcium in the eggshell. All it left behind was the soft part that holds all the egg stuff together. *(Gently remove the shell-less egg from the jar.)* I can't let you hold this because I don't want it to break. But I want you to think: If God made it so that something simple like vinegar can make an egg go from hard to soft, then he can do the same thing with a person's heart. It doesn't matter how bad you've been or how much you hate God. God can take a hard heart and make it into a soft one. A soft heart is one that is good and kind and one that listens to what God has to say. Anyone can have a soft heart, just like anyone here can go home and do this same experiment and end up with a soft egg."

The Science Behind The Sermon

Acetic acid in the vinegar combines with calcium carbonate, the substance that makes up the eggshell, producing a new substance that dissolves in water. After a period of three days, the calcium in the eggshell has been eaten away, leaving only the soft, tough membrane that is always under the shell. It's the membrane that actually holds the yolk (which is food for a developing chick) and egg white (albumen, which serves as a cushion and a source of water for the chick). Once the shell is gone, the membrane holds the whole shebang together.

10

Crushed Cans And Crushed Spirits

The Verse
Psalm 34:18: "The Lord is near to the brokenhearted, and saves the crushed in spirit."

What You Need
hot plate
empty soda can
bowl
ice
water
tongs (the kind that are used to take hot dogs out of boiling water work well)

Some Ideas Of What To Say
(Begin by unloading bag. Hot plate should be plugged in, preferably someplace that little hands can't reach.) "How many of you have been in a hog pile? You know, where everybody piles on top of each other and squishes the person on the bottom. Well, today I want to talk about how you can sometimes feel that way inside. How many of you have ever felt like your feelings got crushed? *(Pour ice with water into bowl, set to one side.)* I know how that feels, too. In fact, everyone here knows what it's like to feel crushed — crushed in spirit. Like when your best friend says she doesn't like you any more or when you lose your absolutely favorite toy and you've looked everywhere to find it. That's feeling crushed in spirit. *(Put a small amount of water into the can and begin heating it as you talk.)* What do you do when you feel crushed in spirit? *(Entertain any reasonable answers. Heat the can until you can see steam rising from it. Chat until you're ready.)* One thing I do when I feel crushed in spirit is go to Jesus in prayer. He says in Psalm

27

34:18 that he 'is near to the brokenhearted, and saves the crushed in spirit.' *(Once the steam is rising, quickly flip the can over into the bowl of ice water. It will collapse very suddenly!)* This can was crushed when the hot plate made all of the air go out of it. That's what can happen when Satan seems to make all the air go out of us. That's when we get a crushed spirit. But God promises that he will SAVE people who have a crushed spirit. All we have to do is ask him to and he will. He'll comfort us. He may not make your best friend come back or your lost toy reappear, but he will love you and be with you. He promised!"

The Science Behind The Sermon

Steam (from the boiling water) takes up more room than the liquid water does and pushes all the air out through the hole. When the can is suddenly cooled, the steam changes back into a liquid again, taking up less space. The leftover space is a vacuum. No air from the outside can get inside. The air pressure inside the can is LOWER than the air pressure outside, so the air outside crushes the can. (This has been done on an old *Newton's Apple* using a 50-gallon oil drum. The effect is the same — though MUCH more dramatic!)

11

Eggs, Inertia, And The Love Of God

The Verse
Romans 8:38-39: "For I am convinced that neither death, nor life, nor angels, nor rulers, nor things present, nor things to come, nor powers, nor height, nor depth, nor anything else in all creation, will be able to separate us from the love of God in Christ Jesus our Lord."

What You Need
1 raw egg (hard-boiled if you're not the daring type)
1 toilet tissue cardboard tube
1 pie tin
1 coffee can
1 small washcloth, hand towel, or small bunch of cloth
1 broom
1 TALL stand or REGULAR-sized table

Some Ideas Of What To Say
(Begin by unloading your bag.) "How much does God love us? *(Set up coffee can, put cloth in bottom of it. Also entertain any reasonable answers.)* A lot, huh? How many of you have seen the movie *Beauty and the Beast*? Remember at the very end, where the beast almost falls off the castle and Belle catches him at the last minute? God is like that. He's there when everything seems like it's falling apart. He's there when life gets hard to live, like when ... *(Relate a personal experience here that kids can understand. Also, set pit tin on top of coffee can. The EDGE of the pie tin should stick out slightly over the edge of whatever table you're using. The COFFEE CAN should NOT stick over the edge! Stand toilet paper tube on end in the center of the pie tin.)*

29

"Today, I want to do a demonstration that shows that no matter what happens to us, God is always there to catch us. Even when the whole world seems to fall out from under us, God is there to catch us. *(Put the egg on the toilet paper tube. Place the edge of the broom slightly under the table. Put your foot on the broom bristles HARD. Pull the broom handle back slightly, aiming at the coffee can/pie tin/toilet paper tube/egg assembly.)* When I let go of this, what do you think is going to happen? *(Accept any response, then let go of the broom. The handle will hit the pie tin. The pie tin and toilet paper tube will fly across the room — and the egg will fall safely into the coffee can, landing gently on the washcloth, unbroken. Expect to be asked to repeat this amazing demonstration. It looks spectacular!)* So the next time you feel that your world has been knocked out from under you, remember that God is always there to catch you!"

The Science Behind The Sermon

According to physics, the egg is a body at rest. Newton's First Law of Motion says that a body will continue to do whatever it WAS doing unless something makes it do otherwise. The broom hits the pie tin, not the egg. Therefore the egg isn't going to move and drops straight down into the coffee can!

12

Diffusion And The Great Commission

The Verse
Matthew 28:19: " 'Go therefore and make disciples of all nations, baptizing them in the name of the Father and of the Son and of the Holy Spirit....' "

What You Need
a strong-smelling liquid (perfume, cologne, or some aromatic oil)
2 mayonnaise jars
a hot plate
water
food coloring

Some Ideas Of What To Say
(Unload and open a bottle of perfume, cinnamon, or other aromatic oil — strongly scented — and leave it alone on your table.) "How many of you know that Jesus told us to go everywhere in the world and tell other people about his love? *(Expect many hands, as well as a few comments.)* What do we call people who go all over the world telling other people about Jesus? *('Missionaries.' Plug in the hot plate and fill a jar with water and place it on the hot plate.)* Did you know that YOU can be a missionary and you don't even have to go anywhere? This demonstration will show you that with the fire of the Holy Spirit living in you, it doesn't matter where you are, you can share the love of God. Some people will go to Africa or South America or to other faraway places. Some people will take a bus downtown to share God's love there. Others will share God's love in their work or school. *(Fill the second jar with water and place it near the first one — but NOT on the hot plate.)* Everybody, take a big sniff. What do you smell? *(Hopefully most will smell whatever it was you brought!)* The smell from my bottle

31

has been spreading all around us the whole time I've been talking. That's like God's love. If it is in you, it will spread. I'm going to show you something else that will show that the Holy Spirit living in you can give you the power to share God's love no matter where you are! This hot plate is going to be like the Holy Spirit, giving lots of energy to the person who wants to share God's love. The jar is the people around you. The other jar is the people around someone who knows God, but maybe aren't as excited about it as they could be. *(Take out food coloring. Blue is best as it is the most visible. Place one drop in each. The food coloring will spread rapidly around the heated jar, much more slowly in the cool jar.)* You can see that for the person who is letting the Holy Spirit work in him, the Good News spreads fast. Pretty soon, it will be all over the place. For the person who isn't letting the Holy Spirit work in him as much — well, the Good News gets spread around, but it takes much longer. We want to make sure that we're like the heated-up jar. We want to make sure that we're doing what God wants us to do."

The Science Behind The Sermon

Convection takes place when a heated fluid, like air or water, rises over the cooler fluid around it. Hot water tends to rise from the bottom of the jar. That rising pushes cooler water ahead of it. You get a current flowing around the jar that carries the food coloring around faster than in the cooler jar. The same holds true for the scent. Convection currents in any place will carry the scent from its point throughout the entire room.

13

Prisms And Promises

The Verse
Genesis 9:12-15: "God said, 'This is the sign of the covenant that I make between me and you and every living creature that is with you, for all future generations: I have set my bow in the clouds, and it shall be a sign of the covenant between me and the earth. When I bring clouds over the earth and the bow is seen in the clouds, I will remember my covenant ... and the waters shall never again become a flood to destroy all flesh.' "

What You Need
a prism
very bright light, like sunlight or a desk lamp narrowed down to a thin slit
darkened room helps

Some Ideas Of What To Say
(Unload your bag.) "Can anybody tell me what happened to Noah? *(Allow any child to describe the events in Genesis. They'll probably all join in.)* Well, you all know that God made a rainbow after the flood. Who can tell me what the rainbow was supposed to mean? *(Let the kids explain it again. If they don't know, you do the storytelling.)* So everybody here knows WHO Noah was, and you know WHY God had him build the ark, and you know WHAT happened after the ark landed on top of the mountain and all the animals came out. But can anyone tell me HOW God made the rainbow? *(See if anyone can explain. The answer here will depend on the age of the kids and whether you have a science whiz among them! Play it for as long as you can. Take out your prism.)* I have here in my bag a prism. Anyone know what a prism does? *(Allow them to tell you.)* A prism splits a beam of light up into colors. Can

anyone tell me HOW it does that? *(You will likely get blank looks here from both the kids and the adults.)* Well, I guess there IS something I can tell you today! Our God is an awesome God to be sure. Because when he made light in the book of Genesis, he made it out of waves. Kind of like the waves on a lake, only invisible to our eyes — unless we split them up. When we use a prism *(demonstrate),* the glass slows down different colors of light waves at different speeds. Red light is the slowest and blue light is the fastest. So when the light comes out of the prism, it's all split up. God made a giant prism in the sky that day — not out of glass, but out of tiny, tiny drops of water. You can make a rainbow when you use a water sprayer on a hose. When you get in just the right place, you can see a rainbow in the air. On the day that Noah and his family came out of the ark, God arranged for them to see a rainbow. It was his promise that he would never flood the earth again. Every time we see rainbows in the sky, we remember God's promise. And now you can remember God's promise any time you want. All you need is a prism, or even a clear plastic pen and a little sunlight.

The Science Behind The Sermon

The science in this one is explained in the sermon itself.

14

Mobius Strips And Eternity

The Verses
John 6:51: " 'I am the living bread that came down from heaven. Whoever eats of this bread will live forever; and the bread that I will give for the life of the world is my flesh.' "

Psalm 100:5: "For the Lord is good; his steadfast love endures forever, and his faithfulness to all generations."

What You Need
a Mobius strip (Take a narrow strip of paper. For demonstration purposes, it should be about four inches wide and two feet long. TWIST IT ONCE and tape the ends together.)
scissors
the plastic cap of a pen
self-sticking, brightly colored dot or sticker

Some Ideas Of What To Say
(Begin by unloading your bag.) "How long is forever? *(Entertain any reasonable answers.)* Eternity is a way that the Bible says 'forever.' Eternity is a long, long time. It's so long, in fact, that nobody on earth can even imagine eternity. Our brains aren't big enough. Let me give you an example. *(Take out the pen cap.)* If I were to make this pen cap a BILLION times bigger, how big would it be? *(Entertain any reasonable answers. It will soon become apparent that this is a difficult concept for children of any age to deal with.)* If I made this pen cap one billion times bigger, the hole in the end would be the size of the earth! Now think — that's only a billion times bigger. What if it were INFINITY bigger? How big would it be? *(Pick up the Mobius strip.)* To give you an idea of how far infinity is and how long eternity is, I'm going to do a trick

with this piece of paper. How many sides does it have? *(Expect them to say two. It's a logical, reasonable answer.)* If it has two sides, then if I put a dot of ink on this side and put my finger on this side, then my finger could never run into the dot, right? *(They should say 'right.' Many will look puzzled.)* Let's try it. *(Put a dot on one side, your finger on the other. Trace a straight line. Soon your finger will come to the dot. Keep going. Soon your finger will arrive at the point you started from — without ever lifting your finger!)* How did that happen? How could my finger get from one side of the paper to the other and then back again? *(Do it again.)* All right, maybe if I try something else. *(Take out scissors.)* If I cut this whole thing in half, I'll have two circles, right? Right. *(Do it and you will have ONE circle. Act puzzled. Most people will have little difficulty acting puzzled!)* This little thing is called a Mobius strip. You can make one by cutting a strip of paper, twisting it once, and taping, gluing, or stapling it together. Then you can do the two things I did. I know this is strange, but it shows me that if a little strip of paper that's twisted once can do things that are amazing, then our God can certainly do the same. He can love us for ever and ever. He will be faithful to us for eternity. And when we die, someday we'll go to heaven and live forever with Jesus. So when you go home today and do a Mobius strip, remember that God loves you forever!"

The Science Behind The Sermon

This little piece of paper is called a topological space. It means that mathematicians have figured out how near a set of points on the strip are — without using numbers. For those of you of an extremely mathematical mindset, the Mobius strip is known as a "nonbounding cycle," since it does not give any boundaries to the surface of the strip. I just think it's neat.

15

Plastic Bags, Pencils, And Abiding Faith

The Verse
Romans 1:16-17: "For I am not ashamed of the gospel; it is the power of God for salvation to everyone who has faith, to the Jew first and also to the Greek. For in it the righteousness of God is revealed through faith for faith; as it is written, 'The one who is righteous will live by faith.' "

What You Need
plastic zipper-lock bag (sandwich size)
pitcher of water
VERY well-sharpened pencil
small plastic wash basin
towels (just in case)
umbrella

Some Ideas Of What To Say
   (Begin by unloading your bag.) "Can anyone tell me what faith is? *(You may get a child who has memorized Hebrews 11:1: 'Faith is the assurance of things hoped for, the conviction of things not seen.' Go with it.)* Faith is believing in something you can't see or touch. Like Jesus. We believe in Jesus even though we can't see him or touch him with our hands. But God has given us a gift — the gift of faith. It helps us believe in those things we can't see. It helps us believe in things even when they seem impossible. *(Take out plastic bag. Fill it with water until it's nearly full, then carefully seal it.)* I'd like to show you how strong this gift of faith is. I'm going to take this pencil and poke it all the way through this bag of water. What do you think is going to happen? *(Entertain as many 'theories' as you want. Most will center around the water gushing out all over the place.)* What would you do if I told you

37

that not a drop of water would leak out of this bag — even if I shoved th epencil all the way through it? *(You may get one or two takers, but the rest will be pretty skeptical.)* What I need is a volunteer to stand under the bag for me while I poke this pencil through it. *(If you can get the pastor, youth director, or other important, well-known personage to stand under the bag, so much the better. Otherwise take who you can get. Make a big show of unfolding the umbrella. Make as if to give it to your victim — then hand it to one of the kids sitting nearest the victim. Make another show of getting the towels ready. If you want to throw on a poncho, go ahead. Get ready. Comment on the amount of faith your victim has. Then puncture the bag directly over his head, LEAVING THE PENCIL IN THE BAG, POKING THROUGH BOTH SIDES. DO NOT PULL IT OUT! No water will leak out. Marvel at the faith of your victim.)* If God has given us enough faith to believe that a simple science trick won't hurt us, then imagine how much faith he's given us to believe in him! Amen!"

The Science Behind The Sermon

The complex polymers that make up everyday plastics have a certain amount of stretch built into them. When you push the pencil through the plastic, the molecules that make up the polymer stretch tightly against the surface of the pencil, holding back the water and essentially plugging the edges of the hole like caulking keeps wind from getting around windows in a house.

16

Vinegar, Soda, And The Holy Spirit

The Verse
Isaiah 61:1: "The spirit of the Lord God is upon me, because the Lord has anointed me; he has sent me to bring good news to the oppressed, to bind up the brokenhearted, to proclaim liberty to the captives, and release to the prisoners."

What You Need
plastic zipper-lock bag (sandwich size) with a smiling face drawn on it
baking soda
food coloring
vinegar

Some Ideas Of What To Say
(Begin by unloading your bag.) "How many of you have heard someone say, 'filled with the Holy Spirit'? *(You may get answers, you may get blank stares. Go with the flow.)* When we talk about being 'filled with the Spirit,' we mean that Jesus is living inside us and giving us the power to do what God wants us to do. Without the Holy Spirit in us, we're not all the way to where God wants us to be. We're kind of limp as Christians. *(Hold up plastic bag.)* Sort of like this bag. Is there anything in it? To show you how God can fill us up with his Spirit, I'm going to add some of this. *(Add about one-fourth cup of baking soda.)* I'll add a couple of drops of this. *(Add food coloring.)* Then, when I'm ready *(get set so you can close the bag quickly once you add the vinegar)*, I add this and BOOM! *(Dump one-half cup of vinegar in and seal the bag. It will fill until it's stiff.)* When you add vinegar to baking soda, it makes a gas called carbon dioxide. It's the same gas you find in a can of soda when you shake it up. Because the bag is closed tight, there's

39

nowhere for the gas to go, so it fills up the bag. Like the gas, the Holy Spirit needs to fill us. When it does, we can walk with God even better than we do now. And instead of being limp plastic bags, we can be full and ready to do whatever God calls us to do."

The Science Behind The Sermon

The vinegar contains acetic acid. The baking soda contains sodium bicarbonate. The two combine in such a way that carbon dioxide (a gas) and water are produced. (For those of you who are chemically inclined: $NaHCO_3$ [sodium bicarbonate] + CH_3CO_2H [acetic acid] = $NaC_2H_3O_2$ [sodium acetate] + CO_2 [carbon dioxide] + H_2O [water].)

18

Popping Bottles And
The Good News Of Jesus Christ

The Verse
Jeremiah 20:9: "If I say 'I will not mention him, or speak any more in his name,' then within me there is something like a burning fire shut up in my bones; I am weary with holding it in, and I cannot."

What You Need
glass bottle (shaped like a wine bottle)
several corks
baking soda
vinegar
funnel

Some Ideas Of What To Say
(Unload your bag and prepare to do the setup immediately.) "How many of you have had to keep a secret? *(This will be a common experience, so you can let the children ramble on for however long you want.)* Have you ever had a secret SO exciting that you could barely keep from telling everyone? *(Add about one-half cup of baking soda through the funnel.)* All right, now — does anyone know what a prophet is? *(Discuss however long you want to here.)* He's a man who has been given a special message from God. He's usually supposed to tell as many people as he can. There was a prophet in the Old Testament and his name was Jeremiah. Jeremiah spoke whatever God told him to say. He was very excited about God. In fact, he was so excited *(Add one cup of vinegar and quickly cork the bottle. This next part requires a bit of timing. If you can, try it a couple of times and see about how long you have before the*

41

cork blows, then you can time your monologue accordingly.), that he wrote in the Bible 'if I say, "I will not mention him or speak any more in his name," then within me there is something like a burning fire shut up in my bones; I am weary with holding it in, and I cannot.' That meant that no matter how hard Jeremiah tried to hold back what God wanted him to say, no matter how hard he tried to hold back how much he loved God and how much God loved him, he couldn't do it. It pushed and pushed until it exploded out of him. *(You want the cork to blow somewhere around here. You may have to ad-lib. But the effect is well worth the effort to achieve!)* All of us want to have God so much in our hearts that we can't wait to tell other people about him. We want to tell other people about the things he does in our lives. When we know how much God loves us, we should be like this cork and bottle and the prophet Jeremiah — about ready to explode!"

The Science Behind The Sermon

The science here is the same as for number sixteen. It's just the end result that's different. Where the bag was flexible (see number fifteen) and able to stretch a bit to hold in the pressure, the glass bottle is NOT flexible. The weakest point of the bottle is the cork. The pressure eventually reaches a point where the friction of the cork against the glass can't hold it in any longer and POW! the cork flies out.

18

A Hammer And A Miracle

The Verse
John 6:19-20: "When they had rowed about three or four miles, they saw Jesus walking on the sea and coming near the boat, and they were terrified. But he said to them, 'It is I; do not be afraid.' "

What You Need
a hammer
string
a WOODEN ruler (plastic bends too easily for this demonstration)
tape
a table edge

Some Ideas Of What To Say
(Begin by unloading your bag.) "How many of you would like to see a miracle? I know I would. Do you remember the time Jesus fed the 5,000? He took a few fish and a couple of loaves of bread and blessed them. Then he fed 5,000 men. That's about ... *(To give you a rough estimate, take the average number of people in your church service and multiply it to find out how many church services it would take to equal 5,000. For example: We have about 300 people per service. The sanctuary holds about 500. So I tell the children how many are in the service. Then I tell them it would take about seventeen churches to make 5,000!)* Can you imagine how surprised the disciples were when Jesus had leftovers? Jesus was God's Son and he did miracles. That was only part of what he did, but it was the part that most people remember. In fact, that was the part of his ministry that the people of Jesus' time remembered, too. They wanted to make him King because of the miracles he did. *(Take out the hammer, tie a loop of string about eighteen inches [46 centimeters] long and tape it midway up the hammer handle.*

43

Slip a ruler through the loop.) Have you ever wondered how Jesus did his miracle? I mean, how did he make enough food for 5,000 people from a few fish and a few loaves of bread? How did he change water into wine at the wedding at Cana? How did he raise Lazarus from the dead? How did he walk on the water? *(Tape the string at the halfway point on the ruler. Place the end of the ruler that is above the hammer head on the table and gently release the hammer. Allow the end of the hammer's handle to press up against the other end of the ruler. Release it. The hammer head should be under the table, the ruler sticking out and only about three to five inches [seven-and-a-half to thirteen centimeters] of ruler holding the whole thing up.)* Jesus performed miracles through the power of God. He WAS God. Lots of people try and explain away the miracles of Jesus. When they can't explain them, they'll try and tell you that the miracles were just made-up stories. But the simple fact is that Jesus was the Son of God. He was with God when God made the Universe. He knew all the rules and he had the power to break all the rules if he wanted to. He didn't do it very often. But when he had to, he did miracles. This hammer hanging here looks like it might almost be a miracle. But it has an easy explanation: it's a science trick. There's an easy explanation for Jesus and his miracles, too. He was the Son of God. We don't need to know any more than that. When he walked on the water, he was showing the disciples that he was the one who had made the world. He could do whatever he needed to do. We believe that Jesus did it — and that's called faith."

The Science Behind The Sermon

Most of the weight of a hammer is in the head. When you move the ruler so that the head of the hammer is directly under the edge of the table, it's as if the hammer were hanging straight down from the table. This is called the center of gravity of your ruler/hammer/string assembly. While it LOOKS impossible, it is a very simple case of balance and gravity.

19

Two Liquids, Two Ice Cubes, And Testing The Spirits

The Verse
1 John 4:1: "Beloved, do not believe every spirit, but test the spirits to see whether they are from God; for many false prophets have gone out into the world."

What You Need
1 small pickle jar half full of rubbing alcohol
1 small pickle jar half full of water
1 ice cube (the larger the better, as long as it will fit in both jars)
water

Some Ideas Of What To Say
(Unload your bag.) "How many of you have ever taken a test? Tests are usually pretty hard. I know all of mine were. But what are tests supposed to be for? *(Entertain all reasonable answers.)* Most tests try to find out what you know. A teacher gives a test to find out who knows what's on the test and who doesn't know it. Then, the teacher can help the person who doesn't know. Tests can also help us figure out what to do with our lives or who we should work with. Tests can help us do a lot of things. I'm going to give you a little test today. *(Hold up the jars with water and alcohol.)* What can you say about these two things? *(Accept all reasonable answers.)* I'll tell you right now that one is poisonous and one isn't. This is the test: how can I tell the difference before drinking them? *(Accept all reasonable answers. One kid will suggest smelling it. Remind them that one is poisonous and the other isn't. Ask, 'What if the smell is poisonous?')* I've got a test I'd like to try here. *(Take out the ice cube. Drop it in the WATER jar first.)* This looks pretty

normal. *(Drop the ice cube in the alcohol jar. The cube will sink to the bottom.)* Whoa! This is different! Now how can you explain this? *(Accept all reasonable answers. Often the kids will say that the ICE CUBE is different!)* Which one should I drink? *(Make as if to drink it — hopefully they chose the water!)* Are you sure this is the right one? *(There should be some hesitation here.)* How could we figure out which one is poisonous? *(Lead them to 'Do some more tests.')* So I should test this before I drink it, right? In 1 John 4:1, John writes: 'Don't believe every spirit, but test them to see whether they are from God....' One of the things we need to do before we choose to follow someone is to 'test the spirits.' We need to see if what that person is asking us to do is something Jesus would want us to do. So we check the Bible, we pray, and ask Jesus to lead us. We test the spirits to find out which one is a spirit we should follow — which one is God's spirit."

The Science Behind The Sermon

Water has a density (density is how close the molecules in a substance are packed) of one (gram per cubic centimeter or g/cc) because water is the standard to which all densities are compared. When water freezes, its density drops, making it slightly lower than water, so frozen water (ice) floats. Alcohol has a density even lower than ice. So when you drop the ice cube into alcohol, it sinks right to the bottom.

46

20

Air And The Assurance Of Faith

The Verse
Hebrews 11:1: "Now faith is the assurance of things hoped for, the conviction of things not seen."

What You Need
meter stick/yard stick
string
2 balloons
2 identical rubber bands
2 identical paper clips
1 pin

Some Ideas Of What To Say
(Unload your bag.) "How many of you believe in invisible things? What are some of those things? *(Steer rapidly away from ghosts! Stick with everyday things like electricity, Jesus, air, and germs.)* Why do you believe in invisible things? If I told you to stick your finger in an electrical plug, would you? Why not? Because you've been taught that there's ELECTRICITY in a socket and it can hurt you, that's why. Believing in something that you can't see is called having FAITH. Most of your parents and grandparents have faith that there's electricity in wires because when you turn on a light switch, the lights always go on. But have you ever been in a house when the electricity has been OFF? What does it feel like to turn on a light switch and have NO power? Pretty scary, huh? I can't do much with electricity, but I can show you a trick with something that you believe in but can't see. Can anyone here SEE air? *(Press for an honest answer. If you live in northern climates, children will point out that you can see your breath in the winter. But that's not air — it's water in your breath*

47

that freezes as soon as it hits the cold air.) I can't see air unless it's very polluted. A long, long time ago, people didn't know about air. They didn't think you needed anything to breathe in order to live. Today I can PROVE to you that air is around you. *(Blow up two balloons. Tie string on the end and hang them from the ends of a meter stick/yard stick. Suspend the stick from a hanger or other stiff wire you dangle from your finger — or the finger of an assistant. Adjust them so the two are balancing.)* Would all of you agree that these two balloons are balanced? So what would happen to the balance if I popped a balloon? *(This may confuse some children — big and little!)* If air IS something, then when I pop the balloon and the whole thing has settled down, the side with the filled balloon should weigh more. *(Pop a balloon. Be sure to warn them about this. I've had crying children when balloons pop!)* I'll pick up these pieces and add them to the stick. And voila! They don't balance any more. Which means that air may be invisible, but it's really there. Electricity may be invisible, but it's really there. And very likely that means that God may be invisible, but.... *(Let them answer.)* Yes! He's really there! The Bible tells us that faith is 'conviction of things not seen.' In other words, by faith we can believe in things we can't see. We believe in electricity, air — and we can believe that Jesus is really there!"

The Science Behind The Sermon

The balloons, paper clips, rubber bands, and string are all balanced. If air weighed nothing, then popping the balloon would have made no difference. But the balance DOES change. Air is made up of molecules of nitrogen, oxygen, carbon dioxide and a few other trace gasses. It has mass and therefore has weight.

A Serious Conclusion

God made the world around us and then gave Adam and Eve the freedom to explore that world. What started with Adam naming the creatures of the earth has taken us to the naming of sub-atomic particles and processes unknown even two years ago. Humans have delved into the heart of the atom as well as into the nucleus of the cell. We have manipulated matter and energy and are now in the process of manipulating our future.

Usually these endeavors are carried out with little regard to the spiritual aspects of the universe. The church, at times antagonistic to science (Galileo Galilei had discovered and announced that the earth was not the center of the universe. As a result, he was held prisoner in his own home by the church until he recanted) and at others nurturing (Gregor Mendel, a Catholic monk, is credited with having discovered the foundations of genetics), has shied away from science.

Science has shied far from faith, preferring to view the universe as a complex collection of undirected phenomena.

This seems a sad waste of talent and effort on both sides.

In this book, I've tried to show that science can illustrate the deeper truths of God and grant a sense of WHY the universe is as it is. In illustrating those deeper truths, science rises from the simple collection of facts to a method of elucidating and clarifying the HOW of the universe.

Science and faith need not remain antagonistic; they can with care and respect come to complement each other.

In doing so, we will all be given a deeper, more glorious understanding of Creation's splendor.

Resources

Books by Janice Van Cleave (various copyright dates, published by John Wiley and Sons):

Gravity
Molecules
Machines
Magnets
Microscopes And Magnifying Glasses
Chemistry For Every Kid
Astronomy For Every Kid
Earth Science For Every Kid
Physics For Every Kid
Biology For Every Kid
202 Oozing, Bubbling, Dripping And Bouncing Experiments
201 Awesome, Magical, Bizarre and Incredible Experiments

333 Science Tricks And Experiments by Robert J. Brown © 1984 TAB Books.
333 More Science Tricks And Experiments by Robert J. Brown © 1984 TAB Books.

Science Works by The Ontario Science Centre © Addison-Wesley Publishing Company.

(AUTHOR'S NOTE: The fifteen books above should put some 2,500 easy experiments and demonstrations at your fingertips — use these plus your own imagination to create endless Science Sermons.)